Can You Survive

THE TITANIC?

An Interactive Survival Adventure

by Allison Lassieur

Consultant:
Norm Lewis
President, Founder, and CEO
Canadian *Titanic* Society
Simcoe, Ontario

CAPSTONE PRESS
a capstone imprint

You Choose Books are published by Capstone Press,
1710 Roe Crest Drive, North Mankato, Minnesota 56003.
www.capstonepub.com

Library of Congress Cataloging-in-Publication Data
Lassieur, Allison.
  Can you survive the titanic? : an interactive survival adventure / by Allison Lassieur.
    p. cm. — (You choose: survival)
  Includes bibliographical references and index.
  Summary: "Describes the fight for survival during the sinking of the ship Titanic"—
Provided by publisher.
  ISBN 978-1-4296-6586-5 (library binding) — ISBN 978-1-4296-7351-8 (paperback)
  1. Titanic (Steamship)—Juvenile literature. 2. Shipwrecks—North Atlantic Ocean—
Juvenile literature. 3. Survival after airplane accidents, shipwrecks, etc.—Juvenile
literature. I. Title.
  G530.T6L37 2012
  910.9163′4—dc22   2011007866

Editorial Credits

Angie Kaelberer, editor; Veronica Correia and Bobbie Nuytten, designers;
   Wanda Winch, media researcher; Laura Manthe, production specialist

Photo Credits

Alamy: Mary Evans Picture Library, 6, World History Archive, 82; The Bridgeman
Art Library International: ©Look and Learn/Private Collection, cover, The Illustrated
London News Picture Library, London, UK, 69; Corbis: Bettmann, 29, Hulton-Deutsch
Collection, 89, 100, Ralph White, 74; Getty Images Inc: AFP/Leon Neal, 71, Hulton
Archive, 27; The Granger Collection, 8-9; Mary Evans Picture Library: Illustrated
London News, 43, National Archives, 53; Painting © Ken Marschall, 10, 12, 21, 35, 44,
58, 65, 103; Shutterstock: pashabo, paper background

Printed in the United States of America in North Mankato, Minnesota.
062014   008276R

TABLE OF CONTENTS

About Your
ADVENTURE

YOU are a passenger on the first voyage of the ocean liner *Titanic*. The ship just hit an iceberg and is beginning to sink. How will you survive?

In this book you'll deal with extreme survival situations. You'll explore how the knowledge you have and the choices you make can mean the difference between life and death.

Chapter One sets the scene. Then you choose which path to read. Follow the directions at the bottom of each page. The choices you make will change your outcome. After you finish one path, go back and read the others for new perspectives and more adventures.

YOU CHOOSE the path
you take through your adventure.

WHITE STAR
LINE

Titanic was as long
as four city blocks.

CHAPTER 1

The Ship of Dreams

It's April 1912. You're thrilled to be traveling on the biggest, most famous ship in the world. The RMS *Titanic* is making her maiden voyage, sailing from England to the United States.

Everything on the ship is better than anything you imagined. Crisp, fresh linens cover the dining room tables, which are set with silver and china. The wood in the magnificent grand staircase gleams. The food is excellent, and there's plenty of it.

Turn the page.

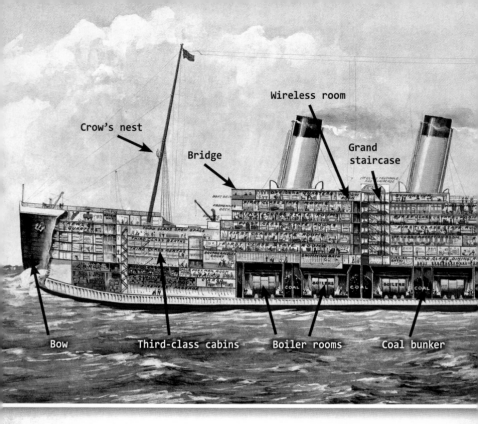

Crow's nest

Bridge

Wireless room

Grand staircase

Bow

Third-class cabins

Boiler rooms

Coal bunker

The ship is also said to be the safest ever built. Its hull is divided into 16 watertight compartments. Devices on the compartment doors will automatically close the doors if water in the compartment reaches a certain height. This feature is designed to keep the water out of the rest of the hull and allow the ship to stay afloat.

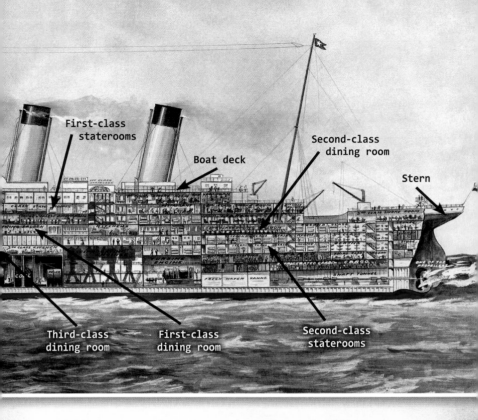

First-class staterooms

Boat deck

Second-class dining room

Stern

Third-class dining room

First-class dining room

Second-class staterooms

The only problem you notice is the number of lifeboats on the deck. There are only 16, plus four collapsible boats. That's enough boats for about half of the 2,200 passengers. But there are life vests in all of the rooms—more than enough for each passenger and crew member.

Turn the page.

Icebergs loomed as *Titanic* sailed south of the Newfoundland coast.

The five-day crossing of the Atlantic Ocean has been smooth. The ship is traveling at an amazing speed of 25 miles per hour. But by Sunday, April 14, you're getting restless. The weather has been good for most of the trip. But this evening, temperatures have dropped below freezing. *Titanic* is scheduled to arrive in New York on Tuesday, April 16. You're ready for this trip to end.

Around 11:40 p.m. Sunday, the huge ship shudders and jerks for a few seconds. Then the gigantic engines fall silent. Stewards appear in the hallways. They urge everyone to put on warm clothing and life vests and go to the upper decks.

Is this a drill? No one seems to know what's going on. Soon you hear dreadful news. The ship has hit an iceberg. Even then everyone is confident that the ship is only slightly damaged. But what if it isn't? Can you make the right choices to survive?

To be part of the crew as a surgeon's assistant, turn to page 13.

To experience the sinking as the governess to a wealthy first-class family, turn to page 45.

To be a 12-year-old boy traveling with your father to New York, turn to page 75.

Titanic's first-class accommodations were the most luxurious at the time.

CHAPTER 2

Serving and Survival

You stand on the deck of *Titanic* and breathe in the cold night air. It's Sunday, April 14. This is the first time you've had a moment to yourself since the ship left Southampton, England, on April 10. You're one of *Titanic*'s medical crew. You are an assistant surgeon to Dr. William O'Loughlin.

When you took the job, you imagined an exciting voyage on the most famous ship in the world. Instead, you've been busy every day tending to the minor hurts and sicknesses of the passengers. You're disappointed that you haven't had more free time. But tonight it seems that everyone is well and safe. You can finally enjoy the amazing ship.

Turn the page.

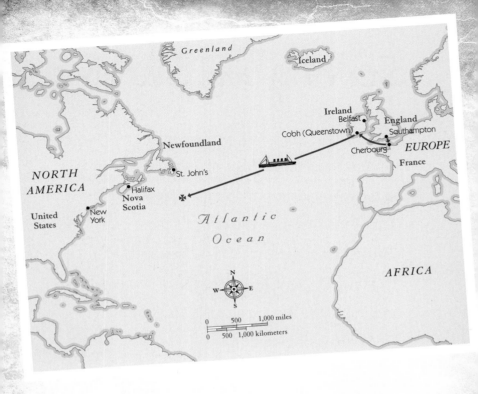

As you look out into the darkness, you think

back to earlier in the evening. You, Dr. O'Loughlin, and several others ate dinner in the first-class dining saloon. You feasted on delicious dishes, such as filet mignon, lamb in mint sauce, roast duckling, and chocolate éclairs. During dinner, everyone talked about how fast the ship was traveling—about 25 miles per hour.

After dinner you wander the decks until around 11 p.m. The weather has turned bitterly cold. You're ready for your warm cabin and bed. You've just fallen asleep when you feel a strange bump. Did the ship hit something? You turn on the light and look at your pocket watch. The time is 11:40 p.m.

Even if the ship has hit something, you're not too concerned. *Titanic* is believed to be unsinkable, after all.

To go back to sleep, turn to page **16.**

To get up to investigate, turn to page **24.**

You turn off the light and drift back to sleep.
A loud knock jerks you awake as Dr. O'Loughlin
steps in.

"What's happened? What time is it?" you ask.

"It's midnight. The ship has struck an iceberg,"
he says calmly. "I need you to come with me. Dress
warmly and bring your life vest."

You quickly put on your clothes, a wool coat,
and a hat. You follow Dr. O'Loughlin to his
quarters. The other surgeon's assistants are there
with Fourth Officer Joseph Boxhall. Everyone is
full of questions.

"Yes, we struck an iceberg," Boxhall says.
"The captain sent me down to inspect the damage,
but I didn't see anything. Sorry, but I must return
to the bridge and give Captain Smith my report."
Boxhall disappears. You notice the ship's engines
have stopped.

"Gentlemen, I have a bad feeling about this," Dr. O'Loughlin begins. "But our first duty is to the passengers. I'll go to second class to make sure everyone is all right there. I need volunteers to do the same in first class and third class."

To volunteer to go to third class, turn to page 18.

To volunteer to go to first class, turn to page 23.

The lower areas of the ship are a maze of narrow hallways and confusing dead ends. But your work has helped you become familiar with the entire ship. You quickly make your way to the third-class lounge. A group of passengers is already there. They look alarmed.

"Doctor, what's happened?" one man asks.

A woman with a baby in her arms says, "I felt a huge bump. Then I heard water rushing in from somewhere."

You tell the passengers what you know. Many of them don't speak English. But you try as best you can to make them understand.

A man comes into the lounge and says, "I heard someone say there's flooding in the boiler rooms. What should we do?"

For the first time you think that the ship is in serious danger. You could brave the bitter cold and go to the deck to find out what is happening. Or you could all stay here in the warmth of the lounge. If the situation is serious, an officer will certainly come and tell you what's going on.

To tell everyone to go up to the deck, turn to page 20.

To advise the passengers to stay put, turn to page 32.

As you start to lead the group out of third class, a crew member appears. You recognize him as John Hart, a steward assigned to this area. "I have orders to send women and children in third class to the boat deck," he says. "I've roused everyone from their cabins. Doctor, help me organize these people. It's a long trip to the deck."

You and Hart take about 30 women and children from the crowd. "The rest of you, wait here," Hart says. "I'll be back."

As he leads the group away, he whispers to you, "These people would never have been able to get out by themselves. Third class is separated from the rest of the ship. There is no direct route to the upper decks." He leads the group on a zigzag route. You walk past the second-class library and down a long hallway past the first-class dining saloon. Then you walk the three flights up the grand staircase to the boat deck.

Passengers who could reach the grand staircase rushed up to the boat deck.

Turn the page.

The boat deck is crowded with people. But no one seems to be in any panic or rush to get into the lifeboats.

Hart helps the shivering third-class women and children into a lifeboat. To Hart's frustration, several of the women jump out of the lifeboat and run inside the warm ship. Finally he shrugs and disappears to get the next group of women and children from third class.

Turn to page 33.

The mood in first class is calm and relaxed. No one seems to realize the danger. You're shocked to see a game of cards going on in the first-class smoking room.

Almost everyone is indoors because it is so cold out on the deck. Several officers are loading people into lifeboats on the boat deck. It's a slow process because no one wants to leave the warmth inside. Many of the boats are launched only half full.

Some people grow bored with waiting and begin to wander back to their rooms. Others urge their families to get into the lifeboats. Your survival instincts tell you that getting into a lifeboat is probably a good idea. Even if this is a false alarm, it's better to be cautious.

Turn to page **33.**

You jump out of bed and get dressed. You don't want to be running around the ship in your nightclothes. Before leaving your room, you grab your life vest.

The hall outside your cabin is quiet and empty. You wonder if you imagined the sound. You see people gathered near the grand staircase. No one seems to be alarmed. Several people are playing cards in the first-class smoking room. One man is hunched over a book. A steward rushes past. You ask him what's going on.

"Nothing to be alarmed about," he replies. "We've struck an iceberg, but it's not serious."

There's some commotion outside on the deck. Part of the deck is covered with chunks of ice. Several young people are playing with them. All that ice on deck makes you nervous, though. You decide to go up to the boat deck. That's where the lifeboats are located.

Once you reach the top of the stairs, you have another decision. Should you go to the port side of the deck or the starboard side? There are lifeboats on both sides.

To go to the port side, turn to page **26.**

To go to the starboard side, turn to page **27.**

There are only a few people on the port side of the deck. But after several minutes, more arrive. Everyone looks as confused as you feel. You spot Second Officer Charles Lightoller and rush up to him.

"Are the lifeboats being launched?" you ask him anxiously.

"Yes, Captain Smith just gave the order," he replies. "But women and children are to be loaded first. I could use your help in loading the passengers."

Turn to page 31.

Not many people are on the starboard side of the deck. But soon the crowd begins to grow. No one seems to know what to do. Just then, First Officer William Murdoch walks up. His face is pale. "The captain's given the order to launch the lifeboats," he tells you. "You had best get in one while you can."

Captain Edward Smith ordered lifeboats launched at 12:25 a.m.

To get into a lifeboat, turn to page 28.

To stay on the ship, turn to page 31.

You help a woman and her teenage daughter into a lifeboat. Then you climb in. Soon all the women and children on the deck near the lifeboat have been loaded, but the boat is not full.

"We can fit more people in here," you call to Murdoch.

"There are no more," he replies. "Launch the lifeboat!"

When the lifeboat is only a few feet above the water, the ropes let go with a jerk. Losing your footing, you teeter and fall over the edge of the boat into the water.

The water is so cold that your brain seems to freeze. Several pairs of hands grab you and haul you back into the lifeboat. Someone throws a woolen blanket over your shoulders.

Many passengers were reluctant to leave the ship for the lifeboats.

"We must get away from the ship," the officer onboard says. "When it sinks, the suction will be so strong that we'll go under the waves with it."

Turn the page.

You're shivering so badly that your hands barely work. But you grab an oar and start to row away from the ship. Several women grab oars as well. It's an oddly calm sight. Orchestra music drifts through the air. All the ship's electric lights are blazing. Everyone on the lifeboat is quiet.

Several women are shaking uncontrollably from the shock and the cold. Most of them only have their nightclothes on beneath their coats and woolen shawls. They probably won't survive this bitter cold for long.

To give your blanket to a passenger, turn to page **36**.

To keep it for yourself, turn to page **38**.

"Women and children must board the lifeboats!" you shout into the crowd. You grab the arm of the first woman you see.

"No, I won't leave my husband!" she cries, clutching the man next to her.

"You must go," you say, pushing her into the lifeboat. You continue to help several more women and children into the lifeboat until the officer yells, "Launch!" You step away and allow the lifeboat to leave without you.

All the lifeboats are gone. The deck is tilting sharply. Deck chairs, tables, and other objects are rolling down the deck and splashing into the water. Maybe there's still a way to survive, if you can somehow keep out of the water. But if you stay on the ship until it sinks, you're likely to be sucked under the waves with it.

To stay on the ship, turn to page 40.

To risk the water, turn to page 42.

"Don't worry, we'll be fine," you reassure the passengers. But minutes pass, and no officer arrives. Finally you decide it's time to get the passengers to the deck.

You lead the crowd through the halls to the first exit. To your horror, the door to the upper deck is locked! Several men try unsuccessfully to break open the door. The panicked passengers rush back through the passageways. But no one seems to know how to get out of the third-class area.

By now the ship is tilted to one side. As the group turns a corner, a wall of seawater roars toward you. You have no time to react as the wall of water rushes over you. It sweeps you and everyone else in the hall to their deaths.

THE END

To follow another path, turn to page 11.
To read the conclusion, turn to page 101.

You walk toward a lifeboat that's nearly full. "Doctor, get into the boat," an officer calls to you. "These people may need medical treatment for the cold."

You step into the boat, and then it's lowered into the water. You and the other men, including a couple of passengers and an officer, grab oars. When you get some distance away from *Titanic*, you look back. The ship's electric lights are blazing. Orchestra music carries across the water. Few people seem to realize the terrible danger they're in.

Over the next hour, *Titanic* sinks faster. People finally realize the danger, but it's too late. There's nothing anyone in your tiny lifeboat can do but watch in horror as *Titanic*'s stern rises higher and higher. Finally the mighty ship breaks in two and falls with a crash. Hundreds of people are thrown into the water.

Turn the page.

You know people can last only a few minutes in such cold water before dying of hypothermia. Sure enough, in less than an hour the screams and moans grow quiet.

You spend the night keeping the other survivors warm. You try not to think about the bodies floating in the icy water just a few feet from the boat.

About 3:30 a.m., the rescue ship *Carpathia* appears on the horizon. Tears of relief fill your eyes as you help the people in your boat board the rescue ship. You're grateful that you all survived, but sad that so many died.

People watched in horror from the lifeboats as *Titanic* went down.

THE END

To follow another path, turn to page 11.
To read the conclusion, turn to page 101.

"Here," you say, draping the blanket over the shoulders of one of the women. The cold air hits you like a slap.

"God bless you, sir," she says through her chattering teeth.

"The most important thing for us right now is to stay as warm as possible," you say to the other passengers. Soon everyone is stomping their feet and rubbing their hands.

Everyone in the lifeboat stares in shock as the stern of *Titanic* rises higher and higher. Hundreds of passengers fall, are thrown, or jump into the freezing black water. The music stops and the electric lights go out for good as *Titanic* pauses, groans, and plunges into the water. The air is filled with the screams of people in the water, begging to be rescued.

"We should go back to get some survivors," you say to the officer. "There's plenty of room in the lifeboat."

"No!" the officer snaps. "If we go back, they will overtake us and cause the boat to capsize. We'll all die."

Finally the sea is silent. You're still wet and shivering. Soon you start to feel sleepy. "I'll just rest a few minutes," you think as you sink to the bottom of the lifeboat. You don't realize that you're suffering from hypothermia. When you close your eyes, it's for the last time.

THE END

To follow another path, turn to page 11.
To read the conclusion, turn to page 101.

You feel ashamed, but you know that using the blanket to stay warm is your best chance for survival. Instead you put your arm around the woman next to you. The two of you huddle together for warmth.

Just beyond the lifeboat, *Titanic* is sinking faster. The ship's stern rises higher and higher out of the water, until its huge propellers are lifted above the waves. Screaming passengers slide down the deck into the water. Others jump. Still more brace themselves against the railing.

One of the huge smokestacks tears apart from the ship and falls to the water with an enormous crash. A few moments later *Titanic* disappears beneath the waves for good. You look away, tears in your eyes.

You know you're lucky to have survived the disaster. Your decision to keep your blanket helped. You and the others on the boat are cold but all alive when the ship *Carpathia* arrives around 3:30 a.m. It's a sight you'll remember for the rest of your life.

THE END

To follow another path, turn to page 11.
To read the conclusion, turn to page 101.

As the ship's stern rises higher, you wrap your arms and legs around the metal rails and hang on. You hear several explosions as the ship slides into the water with alarming speed. You take several deep breaths. Then you jump as far out and away from the sinking ship as you can.

The cold water feels like knives as you are pulled under by the suction of the ship. As hard as you kick, you seem to be going deeper. With a desperate burst of energy, you kick free of the whirling current. You pop out of the water, gasping and coughing, but alive.

Hundreds of people are in the water, frantically splashing and crying, "Help me!" "Save us!" You know that no one is coming to save you. What you must do now is get out of the water. Your chances of dying from hypothermia are much greater in the freezing water.

You spy a wooden table floating nearby and climb onto it. You slowly paddle away, hoping to get clear of the wreckage. Suddenly the table tips and hits you in the head. You're flung back into the water. Unconscious, you float in the water until your frozen body sinks to the bottom of the ocean.

THE END

To follow another path, turn to page 11.
To read the conclusion, turn to page 101.

Holding your breath, you leap as far out into the ocean as you can. The freezing water feels like knives cutting your skin. The water is already filled with hundreds of people screaming for rescue.

You've got to get out of the water before you die of hypothermia. You start swimming. Wreckage is everywhere, but there isn't anything big enough for you to float on. Then you spy a strange sight. About 30 men are standing atop an overturned boat. One of them is Second Officer Charles Lightoller. You swim to the boat and climb aboard.

"We have to stay afloat," Lightoller says. "Everyone stand in two rows along the boat. When a wave rolls us, we can stabilize ourselves."

Through the night you stand with the other men, following Lightoller's orders to "Lean to the left!" "Stand upright!" "Lean to the right!" to keep the upturned boat afloat.

Second Officer Charles Lightoller saved many passengers on his lifeboat.

Soon your wet, frostbitten feet go numb, but you keep standing. Several men collapse and disappear into the water. But you're still standing when the lights of the ship *Carpathia* appear. "We've made it," you whisper hoarsely. Staying awake helped you survive the wreck of *Titanic*.

THE END

To follow another path, turn to page 11.
To read the conclusion, turn to page 101.

First-class passengers swept down the grand staircase on their way to dinner.

CHAPTER 3

Save the Family or Yourself?

You look around at the elegance of *Titanic*'s first-class rooms. You can't believe your good fortune. When you answered the newspaper ad for a governess, you never imagined you'd be traveling on the "Ship of Dreams."

Edward and Annabelle Charles hired you to look after their three children on the voyage. The children are 2-year-old Henry, 6-year-old Agnes, and 12-year-old James. You and the children have spent most of the voyage exploring the ship. It's been great fun.

It's Sunday night, April 14, and you've tucked the children into bed and told them a story. They love your stories about how your brothers helped build this grand ship. Once the children are asleep, you turn off the lamps and go into the main sitting area. Mrs. Charles is there, reading.

"The children are in bed, ma'am," you say.

"Thank you," Mrs. Charles says, smiling. "Why don't you get yourself some dinner? I believe the valets' and maids' dining saloon is still open."

Titanic has a separate dining room for the servants of its wealthy passengers. When you arrive, several servants are eating a late supper. One of them is Rosalie Bidois, Madeleine Astor's maid. Next to Rosalie is Emilie Kreuchen, maid to Elisabeth Walton Robert. Soon you're laughing and talking together.

"I hear the ship is going faster than any other ship!" Emilie exclaims. "We'll surely be in New York before Tuesday."

After the meal you walk about the ship until around 11:30 p.m. By now the weather has turned very cold. You should be getting back. Just as you get to the first-class cabin, the ship jerks slightly. It doesn't feel like much, but it is unusual.

To go into the cabin, turn to page 48.

To return to the decks, turn to page 50.

You forget the slight bump as soon as you get inside the warm cabin. You check on the children. Then you go to your room, a small cabin adjoining the main cabin. Soon you're asleep.

Sometime later a noise awakens you. Something's wrong. The ship's engines have stopped. Mrs. Charles and the children are huddled in the main cabin. Mrs. Charles says, "The steward has ordered us to put on our life vests and get to the boat deck immediately."

"But there's no danger," James says. "Papa said so before he left!"

You nod, trying to look braver than you feel. "Remember what my brothers told me. *Titanic*'s got a one-inch-thick hull and 16 watertight compartments. There's no way it can sink. But let's put on as many warm clothes as we have and do what the steward says, just in case."

"I hate those scratchy wool stockings!" Agnes whines. You put several layers on baby Henry. James is already dressed.

"Wait, I can't leave without my things!" Mrs. Charles cries as she rummages through the luggage, pulling out photos, jewelry, and other personal items.

"We don't have time," you tell her, a hint of panic in your voice.

"I'll only be a moment," she says. "Take the children—I'll be right behind you."

To take the children to the boat deck, turn to page 57.

To wait for Mrs. Charles, turn to page 60.

Your brothers taught you to trust your instincts on a ship. The bump seemed to be from the front of the ship, so you start walking in that direction. You ask the first steward you see what's going on.

"Nothing wrong, ma'am," he says. "Probably dropped a propeller or something." Just as you get ready to return to your room, you spy Emilie. She looks worried.

"We've hit an iceberg," she whispers. "They say we hit up in the front of the ship."

"Let's go see," you say. You're almost to the front of the ship when you realize that the ship's engines have stopped. That's not a good sign. Maybe something has happened to the boilers. "I know where the boiler rooms are," you say. "Follow me!"

You know passengers aren't allowed below decks. But this is an emergency. You and Emilie race down several sets of stairs and passageways toward the bottom of the ship. In the mail room, several postal workers are in knee-deep water. They are scrambling to save bags of mail.

"This is serious," Emilie says. "What do we do?"

The best way to survive a disaster at sea is to get into lifeboats as fast as possible. But maybe the damage isn't as bad as it looks.

To try to find out more, turn to page 52.

To wake the Charles family, turn to page 54.

"I'm not going to wake Mr. and Mrs. Charles unless I'm sure we're in danger," you tell Emilie as you return to the upper deck. "This ship has a one-inch-thick hull and 16 watertight compartments. It's made to withstand a collision like this."

You see one of *Titanic*'s stewardesses, Mary Sloan, speaking to a tall gentleman.

"That's Thomas Andrews," Emilie says, pointing to the man. "He helped design and build *Titanic*."

As you approach Mary and Mr. Andrews, you overhear their conversation.

"Sir, is the ship really in danger?" Mary asks.

"It is very serious, but keep the bad news quiet for fear of panic," Andrews replies. He quickly strides away. Mary disappears as well.

Emilie looks at you in horror. "I must warn Mrs. Robert immediately!" She runs down the hall.

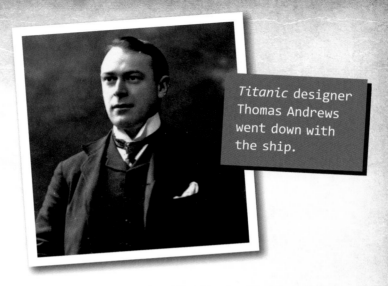

Titanic designer
Thomas Andrews
went down with
the ship.

You have to warn the Charles family. Several stewards and stewardesses are knocking on passengers' cabin doors. Many people are angry at being awakened. Some slam their doors and go back to sleep. Others obey orders and put on life vests. No one seems as panicked as you feel.

You start down a flight of stairs and stop abruptly. The bottom step is underwater. The Charles' cabin is not far. What if they're trapped inside?

To try to get to the cabin, turn to page **63**.

To go back up to the deck, turn to page **64**.

"It's better to be safe than sorry," you think as you go back to the cabin. You tell Mr. and Mrs. Charles what you saw in the mail room.

Mr. Charles looks worried. "Let me talk to the captain," he says. He strides out. When Mr. Charles returns, he looks grim. "We've struck an iceberg," he says. "Let's get the children to the lifeboats." You and Mrs. Charles quickly bundle the children in as many warm layers as you can find. You put on two layers of stockings and an extra sweater under your overcoat.

There's an odd sense of calm on the boat deck when you and the family arrive. A few of the lifeboats have already been launched, but most of them were only half full. No one wants to get into a lifeboat when they can stay warm and dry on the ship.

"You must get in," Mr. Charles says, pushing Mrs. Charles toward the nearest lifeboat. Suddenly the sky is filled with a shower of white stars. Captain Smith has sent out a distress signal. The situation is worse than you thought.

The calm mood turns to panic as people realize the danger. The crowd surges around you, pulling Agnes' hand from your grasp. Frantically you push forward, looking for anyone in the family. But there are too many people! You're holding baby Henry, who starts to cry.

To try to find the family, turn to page 56.

To get into a lifeboat, turn to page 67.

Breaking free of the panicked crowd, you frantically search for the Charles family. By now people are fighting to get in the lifeboats. Several men try to jump into boats, but the officers pull them out.

You see Mr. Charles' black hat above the crowd near the lifeboats on the other side of the ship. With relief you run to him.

"You must get in," Mr. Charles tells his wife. "The lifeboats are almost filled. You don't have much time."

"I'm not going without you!" Mrs. Charles cries.

"Then let the governess take the children into a boat," Mr. Charles says gently.

"No, I will not be separated from the children!" Mrs. Charles is almost hysterical. "We're going back inside where it's warm and dry."

To try to save the children, turn to page 69.

To obey Mrs. Charles, turn to page 71.

You carry Henry and lead the other children to the boat deck. The deck is crowded with confused passengers. Officers are shouting orders. The ship seems to be tilting. There is no sign of Mr. or Mrs. Charles.

"Women and children!" shouts an officer. He sees you and the children. "You there, into the lifeboat!"

"But their mother isn't here!" you cry. "We must wait for her!"

"Get in," a familiar voice says in your ear. Mr. Charles is standing behind you with a grim expression on his face. "I'll see to it Mrs. Charles gets into a lifeboat."

Mr. Charles and the officer help you and the children into the lifeboat. "Papa!" Agnes screams.

Turn the page.

"Don't worry," Mr. Charles says, smiling. "Mama and Papa will see you very soon." Agnes buries her head in your lap as the lifeboat is lowered into the water. The two *Titanic* officers aboard row away from the sinking ship.

Lifeboats 13 and 15 were lowered about 1:30 a.m.

Before long, *Titanic*'s stern rises high into the air. People onboard are thrown into the freezing ocean. You coax the children into singing songs. You hope it will distract them from the terrible screams of the dying passengers. Soon the ship slips below the surface of the sea.

Once the sea is quiet, the children sob themselves to sleep. The night seems to last forever, but the sky gradually begins to brighten. One of the people on the lifeboat gives a shout. A rescue ship is coming!

You don't know if you'll ever see Mr. and Mrs. Charles again, but at least you and the children have survived.

THE END

To follow another path, turn to page 11.
To read the conclusion, turn to page 101.

Mrs. Charles seems to take forever to pack. She tucks the photos and jewelry into a bag. Then she pulls a wad of cash from the safe. "Let's go," she says finally. The small clock on the table reads 1:30 a.m.

"Where's Mr. Charles?" you ask.

"We'll meet him on deck," Mrs. Charles replies. You lead her and the children down the hall toward the main elevator.

"Look," James says, pointing to the end of the hallway. Water is rushing toward the group.

"Follow me," you say, turning around. "I know a different way."

Your brothers spent months working on *Titanic*. They told you about every passageway and ladder in the ship. You herd the family back down the hall as fast as you can. Water laps right behind you.

You run through several more hallways and up a flight of stairs. Finally you reach the aft first-class staircase. With relief you stumble onto the boat deck.

"Where are the lifeboats?" you ask an officer.

"All gone here," he says. "Try the port side of the deck, but be quick."

It's all you can do to drag the children and Mrs. Charles to the port side of the ship. A few boats there are still being loaded. Someone picks you up and throws you and Henry into a lifeboat, along with Mrs. Charles and Agnes. They leave James on deck.

"James must come with me!" Mrs. Charles screams. "He's just a child!"

"No men or big boys," the officer says. Mrs. Charles begins to cry.

Turn the page.

"Jump, James!" you yell, holding out your arms. Before the officer can stop him, James leaps off the deck and into the lifeboat. When the boat reaches the water, two crew members onboard grab oars and start rowing. You're a safe distance from the ship when it slips under the water. You're happy when you are rescued about two hours later.

But you are heartbroken to learn that Mr. Charles went down with the ship.

THE END

To follow another path, turn to page 11.
To read the conclusion, turn to page 101.

The idea of the children being trapped is too much for you to bear. You jump into the water and wade down the hall to the cabin. The door is open, and the cabin is flooded. The Charles' beautiful things are floating everywhere. But thankfully the family is gone.

By now the water is hip-deep. You have trouble getting out of the cabin. If you can make it to the stairs, you'll surely survive. Just as you get there, a wave of water rolls down the hallway. It lifts you off your feet and carries you forward. Something hits your head. You fall unconscious, drowning below decks as *Titanic* sinks.

THE END

To follow another path, turn to page 11.
To read the conclusion, turn to page 101.

When you reach the deck, you scan the crowd for Mrs. Charles and the children. But you don't see them. Officers stand near each lifeboat. They help women and children get in the boats and keep men and older boys away. As you debate which way to go next, James appears in the crowd.

"Blessed be!" you cry, hugging him tightly. "Where's everyone else?"

"Mama and the girls got on a lifeboat," James says, trying not to cry. "They wouldn't let me on because I'm a big boy. I can't find Papa."

You swallow hard. "Let's get on one of these lifeboats, shall we?" you say. "But we'll have to play a little trick on the officers, all right?"

James nods and wipes his eyes. You wrap your shawl tightly around James' head and shoulders, hiding his short hair. Then you push through the crowd to the nearest lifeboat.

"Please let me and my sister on this boat!" you cry to the officer in charge. He barely looks at James as he lifts him up and tosses him gently into the half-full lifeboat. You climb in after James.

As the boat is being lowered, the sky explodes with a bright flash and a loud hiss. "That's a distress signal," you tell James. "We got off *Titanic* just in time."

Titanic's distress signals looked like a fireworks display.

Turn the page.

Several passengers grab oars and start to row away from the ship. Terrible sounds of screaming and tearing metal fill the air, but you can't look. After what seems like forever, everything is quiet.

About 3:30 a.m. a ship named *Carpathia* sails into view. One by one the survivors are lifted onto the ship. Suddenly James shouts, "Mama!" Mrs. Charles has Henry in her arms and is holding Agnes' hand. "Is Mr. Charles here too?" you ask. Mrs. Charles shakes her head sadly. You're grateful that you all survived, but everyone is saddened because Mr. Charles did not.

THE END

To follow another path, turn to page 11.
To read the conclusion, turn to page 101.

"Here, miss," a stranger says, leading you by the arm to a lifeboat. "There's room for you and your baby here."

"Please, sir, the rest of the family is here somewhere!" you cry as the stranger lifts you into the lifeboat. He pats Henry on the head and then disappears into the crowd.

"Mrs. Charles!" you shout. But you can't be heard over the noise as people scramble to get into lifeboats. As the boat is lowered, you look up. The electric lights of the ship are still shining brightly.

Once the lifeboat is in the water, several men begin rowing away from the ship. From here you can see how much of the ship's bow is underwater. "It won't be long now," you think, as you clutch Henry tightly.

Turn the page.

"Hello there," a familiar voice says softly. You turn and see Emilie and Mrs. Robert in the lifeboat with you. "Looks like we survived," is all you manage to say.

"We're the lucky ones," Emilie says sadly. You bury your head in the baby's blanket and pray the rest of the family is as lucky as you two are.

THE END

To follow another path, turn to page 11.
To read the conclusion, turn to page 101.

Quickly Mr. Charles writes something on a piece of paper and hands it to you, along with a roll of cash.

"This is the address of our relatives in America," he whispers. "Make sure the children get to them."

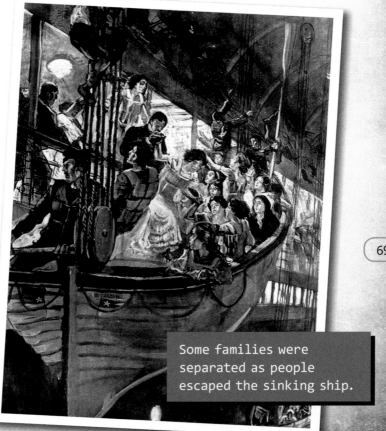

Some families were separated as people escaped the sinking ship.

Turn the page.

You nod. Mr. Charles hands Agnes to the officer in charge of the lifeboat. You clutch Henry as the officer helps you, then James, into the lifeboat.

Mr. Charles tries to persuade Mrs. Charles to join you. She refuses, sobbing. As the boat is lowered, James and Agnes wave tearfully at their parents. Mr. Charles waves back. Mrs. Charles buries her head in her husband's coat.

An hour later it's all over. *Titanic* is gone. All you can think of is that you and the children have survived. You'll do your best to get them to their relatives in the United States.

THE END

To follow another path, turn to page 11.
To read the conclusion, turn to page 101.

You don't think it's a good idea to go back inside, but you must obey your employer. As you pass the grand staircase, you see Thomas Andrews. He helped design and build *Titanic*. He's urging everyone to put on life vests. The deck is tilting now. It's difficult to walk without stumbling.

Life vests kept people afloat in the water, but cold temperatures proved deadly.

Turn the page.

The closer you get to the first-class area, the more a sense of doom fills you. "Please, we must go back to the lifeboats," you beg Mrs. Charles. But she won't listen. "My place is with my husband, and my children's place is with me," she says. The sound of rushing water is coming from somewhere below, but she doesn't seem to notice it.

You know you won't survive if you follow Mrs. Charles. Without a word you turn and run back to the deck. By the time you get there, all the wooden lifeboats are gone.

"I'm not going to panic," you think. Several men have locked arms and made a ring around one of the collapsible boats. They are making sure only women and children get in. You run to the boat and pass through the ring of men. Soon after you get in, the boat is lowered into the water.

Everyone in the boat is silent as you watch the horror unfold. By now *Titanic* is sinking rapidly. People are jumping and falling into the water. The ship's stern lifts out of the water, higher and higher. Then it plunges into the sea and is gone.

About 3:30 a.m. the ship *Carpathia* sails into view. Rescue! You hope the Charles family somehow managed to survive as well.

THE END

To follow another path, turn to page 11.
To read the conclusion, turn to page 101.

Many passengers went on the boat deck to get fresh air.

CHAPTER 4

Be Prepared and Survive

On April 10, 1912, you and your father boarded *Titanic* in Southampton, England. You are headed to New York City. Father has a new job there, and you will get to meet your uncle for the first time. This trip is the first time you've felt happy since your mother's death a year ago.

Father has been busy, so you've spent your time discovering every part of the ship. You've met two other boys near your age and have become good friends. All of you are Boy Scouts, which is a new organization in England and the United States. You also like to get into mischief.

Turn the page.

Today, Sunday, April 14, is no exception. Earlier you tried to sneak into the first-class dining saloon with your friend William Carter, who is traveling first class. But a steward realized you and your other friend, Billy Goodwin, are third-class passengers. He quickly shooed you out.

It's after 11 p.m. now. You're with Father, who is playing cards in the third-class smoking room, and you're bored. You're about to go to your cabin when William and Billy appear.

"I got away when everyone went to sleep," Billy says. "That's not easy when you've got a mother, father, and five brothers and sisters!"

"Mother and my sister Lucile went to bed hours ago. Father is probably in the first-class smoking lounge," William says to you. "Can you get away?"

Nodding, you follow your friends into the passageway outside. "Where shall we go?" Billy asks.

"We could sneak down into the boiler rooms," you suggest.

"I want to see my dog," William says. "We can go to the kennels up on deck."

To go to the boiler rooms, turn to page **78**.

To go to the kennels, turn to page **86**.

The three of you race downstairs until you get to the boiler rooms. *Titanic* has 29 massive boilers that provide power to the ship. Passengers aren't supposed to be in this area. But sometimes you've been able to sneak in before the firemen, who work the boilers, make you leave. You make your way to boiler room 6, which is near the bow of the ship.

Suddenly a metallic tearing sound fills the air. Water starts pouring into the room. An alarm sounds, and a red warning light above the watertight door flashes. Firemen are scrambling around, trying to figure out what's happening.

"Come on boys, follow me!" a fireman shouts. He picks you up one by one and hauls you up a ladder. The fireman barely has time to scramble up the ladder before the boiler room is flooded.

You, your friends, and several firemen lay on the floor of E deck, gasping for breath. "What happened?" you ask.

"Must've hit an iceberg," one of the firemen replies. "Don't worry, though. *Titanic* has 16 watertight compartments. As long as they're closed, the ship will stay afloat. You'd best be getting back to your families."

"A good Boy Scout is observant," you explain. "It's our job to observe what's happening before we report."

The fireman smiles. "You do that, son," he says. "But do it somewhere else. This is no place for children."

To go to the main deck, turn to page **80.**

To go to your father, turn to page **81.**

"Let's go ask Captain Smith what's going on," William says. The three of you go up to the bridge. The ship's commanders are stationed at this area of the ship's bow above the A deck. You know you're not supposed to be in this area, but this could be an emergency.

As you near the bridge, you see Captain Smith with Thomas Andrews, who helped design and build the ship. "We struck an iceberg, and the forepeak and both forward holds are flooded," Andrews says. "The mail room is flooded. Boiler Room 6 is flooded to a depth of 14 feet. Water is coming into Boiler Room 5."

You, Billy, and William look solemnly at each other. You shake hands, knowing you may never see one another again. Then you all rush to break the news to your families.

Father is still playing cards when you run in, breathless. "We've hit an iceberg!" you cry.

Everyone in the room stares at you.

"Nonsense," says an elderly man, turning back to his book.

"I did feel some kind of bump a few minutes ago," another man comments.

"The engines have stopped," Father says, putting down his cards. "Tell me what's going on."

Quickly you tell him what happened.

"All right, son. I believe you," Father says, standing up. "But I'm not sure that it's serious. *Titanic* is practically unsinkable, after all." Father waves to a steward rushing past the lounge and asks him what's going on.

"Put your life vests on immediately, and go to the boat deck," he says impatiently.

Turn the page.

Surprised, Father says, "Do we have time to go back to our cabins?"

"You don't have time for anything," the steward says before rushing off.

"I don't believe him," Father says. "I'm going back for our things. You can come along or meet me on the boat deck."

Many crew members gave their lives to save the ship's passengers.

To go with your father, go to page 83.

To go to the deck, turn to page 85.

The hallway seems to be tilting, and it's hard to walk. In the cabin you put on several layers of woolen clothing and your overcoat.

"Boy Scouts are always prepared!" you exclaim as you grab your pocketknife. Father takes some personal items, money, and a photo of your mother.

Two stewards are banging on doors. They yell for people to put on their life vests. Most people have thrown overcoats over their pajamas. Some return to their cabins and lock the doors.

Third class is a confusing maze of hallways. But you've spent the last four days exploring, so you know every one by heart. "This way to the stairs, Father," you say, leading him down the hall. When you get to the staircase, there's water trickling down it.

*To go up the stairs, turn to page **84**.*

*To go down the hallway, turn to page **91**.*

"This is the shortest way to the deck," you say, ignoring the water on the stairs. "There's no straight way to get to the upper decks from third class. We'll have to go over C deck, then past the second-class library and the first-class dining saloon. Then we'll take the grand staircase to the boat deck."

Father is impressed. "I see you take the Boy Scout rule 'be observant' seriously," he says. "It might just save us."

As you pass the first-class dining saloon, you spot Billy with his family. They look panicked. "Have you seen my little sister Jessie?" Billy asks anxiously. "We were separated. Mother is frantic!"

"We'll help you look," you say.

"No, I'll help them," Father says. "You go to the boat deck and wait. I'll only be a few minutes."

The boat deck is crowded with people. J. Bruce Ismay, the chairman of the White Star Line, is urging passengers to put on their life vests.

"Get into a lifeboat, son," Ismay tells you.

"I can't," you reply. "I'm waiting for my father."

"Then put on this life vest," he says, strapping a life vest over your coat. He then heads toward the bridge. Just then Father appears at your side. "Good boy," he says. "A Boy Scout is obedient, and I see you are too."

The two of you approach a lifeboat. "Women and children only!" the officer shouts.

"I'm with my son," Father calls, pointing to you.

"Sorry, sir, only women and children," he says. "Your son can come aboard."

To get on this lifeboat, turn to page **92**.

To look for another lifeboat, turn to page **93**.

William's dog wags his tail as the three of you pet him. William makes sure the kennel is clean and has plenty of water.

"So what now?" you ask as you leave the kennels. Billy looks out over the deck and gasps, "Look at that!"

Directly in front of the ship is an enormous iceberg. *Titanic* is heading straight for it!

The ship starts to turn away from the iceberg, but bumps against it. A shudder goes though the ship. Huge chunks of ice break off the iceberg and fall onto the lower deck.

"Let's go play in the ice!" William shouts. You all run down to the deck and start throwing big chunks of ice around.

"Hey, the ship has stopped," Billy says. He's right. The engines are quiet.

Just then William's parents and sister appear on deck.

"Boys, come with us," his father says sternly. "They're loading some lifeboats from the promenade deck."

"No, sir," Billy says, "I need to find my family." Billy runs back toward third class.

You follow William's family to the promenade deck, which is enclosed with glass windows. An officer there says, "The captain thinks it will be easier to load some of the boats from here, so you can stay warm. Wait here for further orders."

There's some trouble opening the windows. Everyone is ordered to the boat deck. Then you're ordered back to the promenade deck, then back and forth again! No one seems to know what to do.

Turn the page.

The sky lights up with a white rocket. "That's a distress signal," Mr. Carter says.

"I must find my father!" you say. Mr. Carter grabs you by the shoulders.

"The officers aren't letting men on the boats, but they are loading women and children. If you go look for your father, you will likely not survive."

*To look for Father, go to page **89**.*

*To stay with the Carters, turn to page **95**.*

The boat deck had 16 wooden lifeboats, eight on each side.

"Still, I must try," you insist. Mr. Carter nods and lets you go. You run toward third class as fast as you can, but much of it is underwater now. You're not sure what to do.

"Be prepared," you think, fingering the pocketknife in your coat. "Father would look for me on the boat deck, not on the promenade deck!" You run back upstairs, but it's too late. All the lifeboats are gone. A familiar shape stands beside the railing.

Turn the page.

"Father!" you shout. He turns around and lifts you into his arms.

"We don't have much time," he says. "Our best bet is to stay out of the water for as long as we can. But we don't want to get sucked under with the ship. We can either jump now or wait until the boat goes under."

To jump now, turn to page **97**.

To wait, turn to page **99**.

Father follows you down the hall, which is starting to fill with water. At the top of the stairs is a locked door. Several other third-class passengers are there too. Everyone yells for someone to come, but no one does. The water is coming in faster now.

"I don't think we're going to make it, son," Father says, taking you in his arms. "Don't be afraid. We're together."

You close your eyes and hug Father tight. That's where you are when the water rushes through third class, drowning everyone.

THE END

To follow another path, turn to page 11.
To read the conclusion, turn to page 101.

"I won't leave without you," you say. Father shakes his head. "I'll get on the next boat, son. I'll see you in New York!"

Father hugs you tightly. Reluctantly you climb into the lifeboat with about 20 other people, all women and children. As the boat is lowered, you wave at your father and try not to cry. He smiles and waves back.

The next morning when the ship *Carpathia* rescues you and the other survivors, you search for your father. But you know in your heart you won't find him. You'll be traveling to New York alone.

THE END

To follow another path, turn to page 11.
To read the conclusion, turn to page 101.

Several boats are being loaded, but none of them are filled. "Why aren't they filling the boats?" you ask Father.

"Maybe there are so many lifeboats that they don't need to fill these," Father replies.

"Actually, there are only 20 lifeboats," you reply. "That means that there aren't enough boats for everyone on the ship."

One of the officers spies you and Father. "You there," he calls. "Do you have any experience with boats?"

"Yes," Father responds, surprised. "I sailed in my youth."

"Get on this boat," the officer says. "We need experienced sailors to guide the lifeboats."

Turn the page.

You and Father jump into the boat. After several more passengers are loaded, the officer gives the order to lower the boat. Once you're on the water, Father takes charge. He shows the others how to row the lifeboat.

There's nothing to do now but watch the great ship sink. It's a horrible sight as hundreds of people are thrown into the freezing water. *Titanic* finally slides into the ocean and is gone for good. After about 30 minutes the screams grow quiet. Now there's nothing to do but try to stay warm and wait for rescue. At least you and Father have survived.

THE END

To follow another path, turn to page 11.
To read the conclusion, turn to page 101.

Finally the officers get the windows open and Boat 4 in position. They stack deck chairs next to the window so people can climb out into the lifeboat. Officer Charles Lightoller helps you, William, Lucile, and Mrs. Carter into the boat. They wave tearfully to Mr. Carter.

Lightoller orders the boat to be lowered. By now *Titanic* has sunk so far that the lifeboat only drops a few feet before it hits the water. Two crew members row as hard as they can to get away from the ship before it sinks.

You don't know how you make it through the terrible, cold night. You and William take turns pounding on each other's feet and legs to keep warm. About 3:30 a.m. a ship appears on the horizon. It's the *Carpathia*. You're hauled up to the ship with a rope. An officer takes your name. "Go into the dining saloon. There's hot soup for everyone there," he says kindly.

Turn the page.

You are stumbling toward the dining saloon when suddenly you're caught up in a bone-crushing hug. "Father," you gasp.

"When the ship went down, I climbed onto some wreckage. A lifeboat picked me up," Father explains.

Later you find out that Billy's family didn't survive the sinking. So many people died. You and Father are two of the lucky survivors.

THE END

To follow another path, turn to page 11.
To read the conclusion, turn to page 101.

"Let's go now," you say.

"All right. When I tell you to go, jump with me."

You stand at the railing with Father as the ship tilts farther upward. Soon you can't keep your footing. The seawater is rushing toward you when Father yells, "Take a deep breath, and jump as far as you can. I'll be right with you!"

The cold water tears through you with a pain you've never felt before. You barely hold your breath long enough to get to the surface.

The water is filled with wreckage. There's a tangle of ropes and heavy wooden doors in front of you. Your frozen fingers somehow open the pocketknife. You saw at the ropes until they loosen, and one of the doors breaks free. Painfully you climb onto it.

Turn the page.

"Father!" you shout until you become hoarse, but you can't see him. Some time later a lifeboat appears, and several strong hands haul you up. You feel frozen, but not just from the cold. You've survived, but Father is gone forever.

THE END

To follow another path, turn to page 11.
To read the conclusion, turn to page 101.

The stern rises higher in the air until the ship is straight up. Screaming passengers tumble past you. The ship balances for a moment. Then it begins to plunge into the water.

"Take my hand!" Father yells. Father jumps and pulls you with him. The water is unbelievably cold, but you manage to hold your breath. You're pulled under. You fight your way to the surface, still clasping Father's hand.

Together you start swimming, hanging onto floating wreckage. A lifeboat appears in the darkness. With all the strength you have left, you paddle toward it. Rough hands grab you and pull you up. Someone throws a blanket around you.

"You and your father are lucky to survive," a voice says. "You'll be fine now."

THE END

To follow another path, turn to page 11.
To read the conclusion, turn to page 101.

Titanic survivors gathered together after their rescue.

CHAPTER 5

Why Did Some Survive?

Of more than 2,200 people on *Titanic* on that terrible night, only 705 survived. Survival depended on many things. Most people survived by luck, but a few understood what was happening and made the right choices.

More third-class passengers—about 536—died than any other class. Several things worked against them. Many third-class cabins were in the bow of the ship. They were the first to flood when the ship hit the iceberg.

The third-class area was also separated from the rest of the ship. This was because of fears that third-class passengers would carry diseases. On *Titanic* many third-class passengers couldn't find their way out to the lifeboats. Also, some third-class passengers didn't speak English. They couldn't understand the crew members' instructions.

First- and second-class passengers were more likely to survive, but only women and children. The idea of "women and children first" was a strong one at the time of the disaster. Many survivors told stories of how men sacrificed themselves so that women and children could live.

Passengers who understood the danger early were more likely to live. When *Titanic*'s officers began loading the lifeboats, few passengers were willing to leave the warm ship. Most lifeboats were only partially filled when they launched. By the time the rest of the passengers realized the danger, it was too late.

Water rushed over the grand staircase as *Titanic* sank.

For male passengers, the side of the boat deck they went to made a difference. Second Officer Charles Lightoller supervised the lifeboat boarding on the port side of the deck. He allowed few men to board these boats. First Officer William Murdoch supervised the boarding of boats on the starboard side. He allowed more men to board.

More than 1,500 people went into the water when *Titanic* sank. As many as 1,000 were probably still alive. The key to survival was to quickly get out of the freezing ocean water. *Titanic*'s lifeboats did rescue a few people from the water. Most of these people lived.

The woolen clothing commonly worn at the time of the disaster also helped people survive, especially if they went into the water. Wet wool acts as an insulator. It keeps skin warmer than the synthetic fabrics people wear today.

The *Titanic* disaster shocked the world. The biggest reason so many died was the lack of lifeboats. Also, there were no standard rules for getting passengers off the ship during an emergency.

Today the world is still interested in *Titanic*. Movies, books, TV shows, and plays tell the story of that desperate night and the people who survived it—and those who didn't.

REAL SURVIVORS

William Carter—Eleven-year-old William Carter
was traveling first-class with his parents and older sister.
He, his mother, and sister all survived the sinking,
even though the crew member loading the lifeboat
at first refused to let him on. The crew member also
refused to let William bring his dog, which upset him
very much. Millionaire businessman John Jacob Astor
comforted William by telling him he would take care
of the dog. Both Astor and the dog died in the disaster.
Unfortunately, William's friend Billy Goodwin also died,
along with his entire family.

Emilie Kreuchen and Rosalie Bidois—Ladies'
maids Emilie Kreuchen and Rosalie Bidois boarded
lifeboats with their employers, Elisabeth Walton
Robert and Madeleine Astor. All four women survived
the disaster.

Margaret Brown—Margaret Brown was a wealthy
woman traveling with her friends, John Jacob and
Madeleine Astor. She is famous for helping load other
passengers into lifeboats and for encouraging the other
women in her boat to join her in rowing to safety. After
the disaster, she set up a fund for *Titanic* survivors and
worked to win women the right to vote. She died in 1932.

Millvina Dean—At 2 months, 27 days old, Millvina Dean was the youngest passenger on *Titanic*. She and her older brother were traveling third-class with their parents to the United States. Her father planned to open a store in Wichita, Kansas. Dean, her mother, and her brother survived, but her father died. The family returned to England, where Dean lived until she died May 31, 2009, at age 97. She was the last living survivor of the *Titanic* sinking.

SURVIVAL QUIZ

1. When you learned that the ship struck the iceberg, what was the best thing to do?

(A.) Put on your life vest and warm clothes and go up to the deck.

B. Stay in your cabin and wait for further instructions.

C. Make sure all of your possessions are safe.

2. What was the smartest thing to do when boarding a lifeboat?

A. Wait on deck to see if the situation is really serious before boarding a boat.

B. Try to find your family or friends to make sure that you get on the same lifeboat.

(C.) Get on a lifeboat right away, and row away from the ship.

3. If you ended up in the water, what was the best thing to do?

A. Tread water.

(B.) Swim to a lifeboat as quickly as possible.

C. Grab onto a piece of debris and float on it until the rescue ship comes.

Answers: A, C, B

READ MORE

Adams, Simon. *Titanic.* New York: DK Pub., 2009.

Benoit, Peter. *The Titanic Disaster.* New York: Children's Press, 2011.

Brown, Don. *All Stations! Distress! April 15, 1912: The Day the Titanic Sank.* New York: Flash Point/ Roaring Brook Press, 2008.

Temple, Bob. *The Titanic: An Interactive History Adventure.* Mankato, Minn.: Capstone Press, 2008.

INTERNET SITES

Use FactHound to find Internet sites related to this book. All of the sites on FactHound have been researched by our staff.

Here's all you do:
Visit *www.facthound.com*
Type in this code: 9781429665865

Glossary

aft (AFT)—toward the back of a ship

boiler (BOY-luhr)—a tank that boils water to produce steam

bow (BOH)—the front end of a ship

collapsible (ke-LAPS-eh-buhl)—a type of lifeboat with folding canvas sides

governess (GUH-vur-nuss)—a woman who cares for and teaches children in their home

hull (HUHL)—the main body of a ship

hypothermia (hye-puh-THUR-mee-uh)—a condition that occurs when a person's body temperature falls several degrees below normal; hypothermia can be fatal if not treated

orchestra (OR-kuh-struh)—a large group of musicians who perform together

saloon (suh-LOON)—a dining or lounge area

stern (STURN)—the back end of a ship

steward (STOO-urd)—the ship's officer who is in charge of food and meals; a steward is also an attendant on a ship

BIBLIOGRAPHY

Barratt, Nick. *Lost Voices from the Titanic: The Definitive Oral History.* New York: Palgrave Macmillan, 2010.

Butler, Daniel Allen. *Unsinkable: The Full Story of the RMS Titanic.* Mechanicsburg, Pa.: Stackpole Books, 1998.

Encyclopedia Titanica. 11 April 2011. www.encyclopedia-titanica.org

Expedition Titanic. 11 April 2011. www.expeditiontitanic.com

Inside the RMS Titanic. 11 April 2011. www.titanicandco.com/inside.html

Lord, Walter. *A Night to Remember.* New York: Holt, 1955.

Merideth, Lee W. *1912 Facts about Titanic.* Sunnyvale, Calif.: Rocklin Press, 2003.

Mowbray, Jay Henry, ed. *Sinking of the Titanic: Eyewitness Accounts.* Mineola, N.Y.: Dover Publications, 1998.

Titanic Historical Society, Inc. 11 April 2011. www.Titanic1.org

Winocour, Jack, ed. *The Story of the Titanic, as Told by Its Survivors.* New York: Dover, 1960.

INDEX